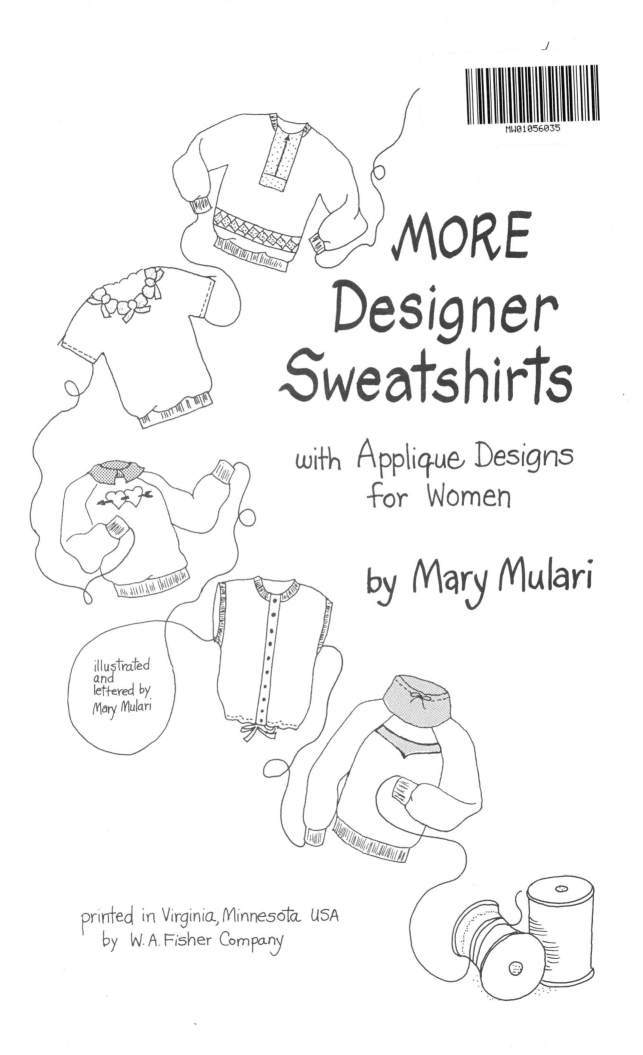

MORE
Designer
Sweatshirts

with Applique Designs for Women

by Mary Mulari

illustrated
and
lettered by
Mary Mulari

printed in Virginia, Minnesota USA
by W.A. Fisher Company

With Special Thanks to

My "Board of Directors" and models:

Joyce Banttari   Nancy Johnson
Karen Buell   Karen Kellogg
Margaret Croswell   Theresa Miklausich
Nancy Harp   Lil Moscatelli
Dorothy Jamnick   Sandy Nemanic

Thanks for cooperation and assistance from:

Sharon Kerssen
Lois Mattson
Kate Croswell

Photography by Margaret Croswell

ISBN 0-9613569-4-4

Eighth Printing: November 1992

Table of Contents

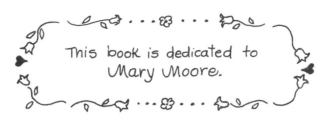

This book is dedicated to
Mary Moore.

Opening Remarks

to the Good and Gentle
Readers of this book

Welcome to another collection of ideas for designer sweatshirts.

I hope you are familiar with and using many of the newer sewing tools that help to make sewing a pleasure :

· ⌇ washable marking pens ~·
· ⌇ Stitch Witchery™~·
· ⌇ gluestick ~·
·~ tear-away stabilizer for ~· applique work

Another important tool is the iron. While your sewing machine is on, the iron should also be on and used frequently. The pay-off is a designer sweatshirt with a professional look.

Two methods of preparing appliques are described on pages 28-29. Read about and try these techniques and materials to create appliques with a first-class appearance.

The world of sewing is continually expanding with new equipment and ideas. I am encouraged by the number of stitchers who are eager to learn about what is new. To have an open mind and enthusiasm for sewing is healthy for all of us.

gluestick

Fray-check™

Fray Check™

stitch witchery™

Stitch N Tear Pellon®

iron

marking pens

purple marking pen

blue marking pen

applique pressing sheet

applique scissors

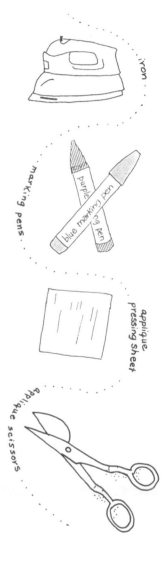

may you always sew with a happy heart

Introduction -- or How I Came to Write Another Book

First there was the craft show that featured decorated sweat-shirts. It was a source of inspiration and the beginning of a class I developed and named "Designer Sweatshirts." Then in 1983 I published my first book based on the class ideas. DESIGNER SWEATSHIRTS became a self-publisher's dream when the copies sold quickly and the response was enthusiastic. From the day the book was released, many have asked me, "What's your next book going to be about?" I was shocked because I had no plans for further writing and anyway, wasn't one book enough? (Do they ask the same question of couples who have one child?)

In continuing to teach and present seminars I found that the ideas and inspiration did not end. Soon one book was not enough. APPLIQUE DESIGN COLLECTION was published in 1984 as a resource book of applique patterns. Now it is time to present more suggestions for decorating sweatshirts, still favorite garments for warmth and comfort. Of course, many of these ideas can be applied to other garments. If you can use the information in this book to imagine and develop your own creations, I will be encouraged and pleased.

A special section of this book, "Applique Designs for Women," begins on page 31. This is a category of designs for which I have had many requests. Many designs are available for children but women look for different ideas for themselves, for designs appropriate to their age and personal style. May these designs inspire you to stitch many unique applique projects.

And now, let's begin to explore the possibilities for more designer sweatshirts · · ·

Ruffled Neckline and Placket
(pictured on front cover)

Supplies needed: one crewneck sweatshirt with raglan sleeves
~ 1/3 - 1/2 yard fabric for ruffle, placket and other details
~ 3 to 5 buttons 1/2" in diameter

1. Determine the length of the placket on the raglan seam line of the sweatshirt and place a pin across the bottom. The placket on the cover shirt is approximately 6" long.

2. Measure length of placket and all around the top of the neckline ribbing. (Hint: Stand the tape measure on edge to get an accurate measurement. Do not stretch ribbing.) You will be adding a ruffle of this length to the placket and neckline. Double this measurement to determine length of fabric needed for the ruffle. Cut a piece of fabric of that length and 2 1/4" - 2 1/2" wide. Fold the fabric in half lengthwise, iron, and gather on the cut edges. From the same fabric, cut a piece of bias tape 3/4" wide the length of the neckline circumference only. Double the placket length, add 2 inches and then cut a placket piece of that length and 3 1/4" wide.

3. Staystitch placket opening by sewing slightly less than 1/4" on each side of raglan seam. Sew back and forth across the bottom for reinforcement. Then cut the placket open on the raglan seam between the stitching lines.

4. Pin gathered ruffle into placket opening, starting at bottom of opening and continuing around the neckline. The cut edges of the ruffle line up with the edge of placket opening and top of neck ribbing. Pin bias tape (right side of tape down) over the ruffle in neckline only. Stitch ruffle and bias in place with 1/4" seam.

5. Turn under and iron the other, loose edge of the bias. Adjust ruffle to stand up in neckline and pin bias tape onto the ribbing inside the neckline. Hand stitch the edge of bias tape into place to avoid a visible seam through the ribbing. →

6. Iron placket fabric in half lengthwise. Also turn back the 2 long edges and iron. Mark the center of the placket's length and pin that mark to the bottom of the placket opening. Pin placket in place up each side of the opening, inserting edge of sweatshirt inside fabric placket about 1/4." Stitch fabric placket onto sweatshirt in one continuous seam, spreading the opening wide when you stitch across the bottom. Trim and turn under the top edges of placket fabric. Before stitching the top edges in place, you may wish to trim away the fabric bulk on the ruffle side in order to stitch a buttonhole through the ribbing. (Now lean back and sigh - you're nearly done.)

7. Sew in buttonholes and buttons to close the placket opening. Buttons covered with the ruffle fabric add a nice detail. The Maxant brand of covered buttons is recommended. Velcro may be used instead of buttons and buttonholes or used in combination with buttons stitched on the front of the shirt.

Options: - You may substitute gathered eyelet lace for the ruffle.

- Place the ruffle down the center front of the shirt or down both raglan seams
- Make a bias ruffle using the instructions on the next page.

About the shirt on the cover of this book:

The ruffle, covered buttons and appliques make use of pindot fabrics. The exact strawberry and flower shapes can be found in my book *APPLIQUE DESIGN COLLECTION*. The vines were created with narrow rickrack.

You can use the strawberry on the left and the designs on page 8 to create a pleasing arrangement of appliques similar to the cover sweatshirt.

A Bias Ruffle for Ruffled Neckline Sweatshirts

To produce a bias strip of fabric long and wide enough for a ruffle on any adult size sweatshirt, use the following directions. This method allows the use of a minimum amount of fabric and avoids the "stringy" edges of ruffles cut lengthwise or crosswise on fabric.

 1. Cut 1 - 10" square of fabric.

2. Cut square into 2 triangles.

 3. Line up 2 sides of triangles and stitch across, using 1/4" seam allowance.

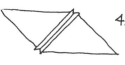 4. Press seam open. With wrong side of fabric up, divide the fabric into 3 equal sections, approx. 2 3/8" wide. Draw lines on fabric with a washable marking pen.

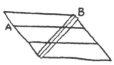 5. Form a tube by bringing point A to point B. (Right side of fabric inside.)

 Pin 2 edges of fabric together and stitch with 1/4" seam allowance. Press seam open.

6. 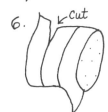 Begin cutting bias at place marked by arrow and continue cutting to end of the tube.

There will be several seams in this bias strip but when it is folded in half lengthwise for the ruffle, the seams will not meet others and create bulk. If you use a small print, the seams will not be noticed.

Happy Ruffling —
with no "strings" attached!

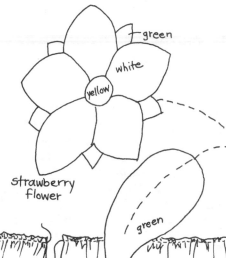

strawberry flower

dashed lines indicate stitching lines

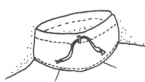

Cowl Drawstring Collar

Replace the neck ribbing on a plain sweatshirt with a larger open collar with a drawstring. The collar fabric can be a print to coordinate with the sweatshirt color or a solid color to match the shirt.

Measure and mark 1" below the neck ribbing all around the neckline. Stitch around the neckline on the marks. This will be staystitching to retain the shape of the neckline. Cut away the ribbing and sweatshirt fabric 1/4" above the stitching line.

Measure the distance around the staystitching by using the edge of a tapemeasure. Add 1/2" to the measurement for seam allowances. Cut the collar fabric to this length and 8" wide. (Approximately half of the 8" will be the finished collar's width so adjust this measurement if you want a "taller" or "shorter" collar.)

Fold the fabric in half lengthwise and widthwise as the dashed lines A + B indicate. Iron these folds for guides and then open fabric flat again.

At center front on line B and immediately below line A, stitch a small buttonhole 1/2" long or insert a grommet opening on the right side of the fabric.

Stitch the sides of the collar fabric together to form a tube. Use 1/4" seam allowances. Turn under 1/4" and iron the top and bottom edges of the tube. Fold the tube in half on fold A with wrong sides of fabric inside.

Fit collar into neck by placing sweatshirt neckline in between the pressed edges of the collar tube. Pin the edges of the collar over the staystitching. Place the seam of the collar at the shirt's center back. Sew the collar in place by sewing through all layers from the right side of the sweatshirt.

Pin the fold in place around the top of the collar. Form a casing by stitching the collar together below the bottom of the buttonhole. String a ribbon, braid, or fabric tie through the casing.

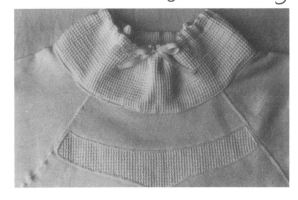

Knit Collars and Turtlenecks

To create the look of layered clothing with a sweatshirt, consider sewing a knit collar or turtleneck piece inside the neck of a sweatshirt. For many sweatshirt wearers, one layer of clothing is enough but the look of layers is desirable and interesting.

Sandy and Karen in sweatshirts with attached collars.

Knit collars can be purchased at fabric shops. Select one appropriately sized for an adult or child. Pin the front edges of the collar inside the neck at center front. Wrong side of collar will be against the inside of sweatshirt neck. Keep all pins on the sweatshirt's right side. Make sure that the bottom edge of the collar is pinned over the "ditch" between the ribbing and the body of the shirt. Pin the center back of the collar to center back of the shirt and over the "ditch." Then pin the rest of the collar into the neckline of the shirt, stretching collar slightly, if necessary.

center front

ditch

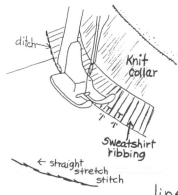

ditch

Knit Collar

Sweatshirt ribbing

← straight stretch stitch

Use thread to match the sweatshirt color as the top thread. Bobbin thread can match collar color. Adjust the sewing machine to the straight STRETCH stitch. Sew on the right side of the sweatshirt in the "ditch" so the stitching line will not be visible. Since you have carefully pinned the edge of the collar over the ditch inside the neckline, you will now be sewing the collar into the sweatshirt's neckline. The neckline must "give" so a head can be pulled through so we use a STRETCH stitch to maintain the expansion of the neckline.

Now let's try adding a turtleneck—

Here's how to get the look of a separate turtleneck shirt worn under a sweatshirt:

1. Select a lightweight knit fabric -- interlock knit or ribbed knit -- for the turtleneck piece you will sew into the sweatshirt neckline. You can determine the size of the neck piece by measuring a turtleneck shirt that fits well. The length will be 10"-12" for an adult, depending on the amount you wish to turn down in the neck. Stretch the knit fabric around your head to determine the width of the neck piece. Then cut the knit fabric to your dimensions.

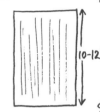

2. With right side of knit fabric inside, pin the sides of the fabric together and sew the fabric into a tube. Fold the tube in half by bringing the cut edges of fabric together with right sides of fabric on the outside.

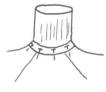

3. Pin the turtleneck cut edges inside the sweatshirt neckline. Center the seams of the "tube" over the ditch at center back of shirt. Next, pin the center front of "tube" over the ditch at shirt center front. Pin turtleneck tube to fit into the rest of the neckline, keeping all pins on the outside of the shirt.

4. Stitch turtleneck onto the shirt with straight STRETCH stitch. Top thread will match sweatshirt and you will be stitching in the "ditch" as with the knit collar on the previous page.

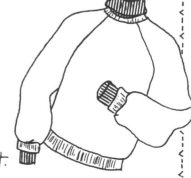

You can also add "fake" cuffs to the bottoms of sweatshirt sleeves using this same method. This second pair of cuffs will give more evidence of "layering" without the added bulk of a second garment.

Quilting on Sweatshirts

Hand quilting around a design on the front of a sweatshirt adds a special look. This decoration is subtle and a choice of many women who prefer to decorate with softer designs.

Supplies you'll need : thin but fluffy quilt batting, light weight muslin, thread for basting & quilting

1. Select a quilting design or combine some shapes into a pleasing arrangement. The design on the back cover of this book could be used. Cut the design from paper or use a quilting template. Carefully trace the design onto the shirt with a washable marker.

Stitching through the shirt, batting, and muslin creates the puffy look of trapunto quilting — a soft and subtle decoration.

2. Cut a piece of batting a little larger than the design area. Also cut a piece of muslin or lightweight cotton fabric the size of the batting. Pin the batting, then the muslin on the wrong side of sweatshirt and beneath the design area.

3. Carefully baste the batting & muslin to the sweatshirt from the right side of the shirt. Begin basting in CENTER of design and stitch through all 3 layers to the edges of the batting below. Tie knots at both ends of stitching. Baste at least 4 lines of stitching as shown in the diagram.

4. Begin quilting. Select a thread color to match or contrast and use one strand. Sew small, neat stitches along the lines drawn on the shirt. Plan to stitch from the center out to the edges of the design. You will stitch through shirt, batting, and muslin.

5. Remove basting threads carefully. On the back of the shirt you may trim away some of the excess batting and muslin. Wet the shirt front to remove the lines drawn with the marker.

  ⌣ This decoration is a great idea for a friend who quilts.
  ⌣ Consider using perle cotton for the quilting.

Sweatshirt Inserts — Just for Fun or to Alter a Sweatshirt

In case a sweatshirt is never long or short enough to suit your shape, you can improve the situation with inserts. And, you can add inserts even if you don't have a fitting problem to correct.

An insert can be a strip of fabric to match the sweatshirt color, a strip of Seminole Patchwork as shown above, a strip of contrasting color fleece or any fabric as washable and durable as the shirt.

Determine the length for the insert by measuring around the sweatshirt body (or sleeve) above the ribbing. Decide on the width of the insert. Add ½" to both the length and width measurements to allow for seams. Cut the insert and sew it into a tube, using ¼" seam allowances.

Now let's prepare the shirt. Measure up from the top of the ribbing to a distance you wish to locate the bottom of the insert fabric. 2" or 3" might be a suitable distance. Place marks all around the shirt body or sleeve.

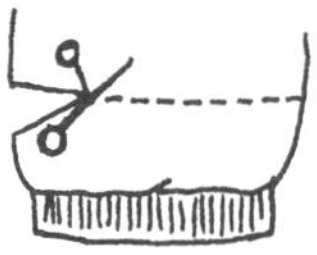

Insert the scissor tip through the shirt on one of the marks and cut carefully around the shirt, removing the bottom of the shirt. Pin right side of bottom edge of fabric insert to right side of shirt section with ribbing attached to it. Place the seam on the insert at the side or center back of sweatshirt. Stitch the insert onto this part of the shirt with ¼" seam allowance.

For LENGTHENING a shirt, pin and stitch the top edge of the insert to raw edge of upper shirt, right side of fabric to right side of shirt. The sweatshirt will be lengthened by the width of the inserted fabric.

To SHORTEN with the insert, plan to cut away part of the shirt body. Remember that you will sew on an insert of __" width so cut at least that much from the shirt in order to shorten it. After cutting, attach the top edge of the insert to the top section of shirt body.

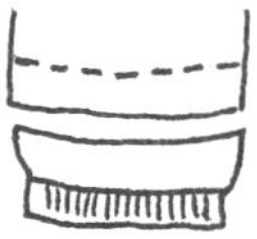

To MAINTAIN the shirt's original size, cut a piece off the shirt's top section. The piece will be ½" less than the width of the insert to allow for seam allowance.

You may increase the width of the seam allowances and/or reinforce the insert and sweatshirt seam edges if you wish.

Credit goes to Ellie Werner for the first sweatshirt with Seminole Patchwork inserts.

13

Zippered Neckline

Nancy's sweatshirt features a zippered neck opening and a pieced insert to lengthen the shirt.

Add a zipper to the neckline of a crewneck sweatshirt. This variation becomes a decorative way to open a neckline with fabric strips added to the sides of the zipper.

Select a 7" or 9" zipper or another length of your choice. Prewash zipper and fabric chosen for trim.

Cut 2 fabric strips for the sides of the zipper at least 2" longer than the zipper. The width could be 2" or a measurement of your choice.

Place one strip in place on one side of zipper with right side of fabric to right side of zipper. Match fabric and zipper at bottom of zipper tape. Extend extra fabric beyond top of zipper. Stitch in place with zipper foot on machine. Sew fabric strip to the other side of zipper in the same way.

Across the bottom of the fabric strips and zipper, below the stopper bar, stitch another strip of fabric.

Turn under and iron the sides and bottom of the fabric trim. Zipper with attached fabric can now be sewn into the sweatshirt neckline.

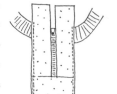

Position zipper placket on sweatshirt center front, raglan seam or at shoulder center line. Top of zipper teeth should be lined up with top edge of neck ribbing. Pin into place.

Sew the zipper placket onto the shirt by stitching on sides and across bottom.

Trim away some of the extra fabric at the top of the zipper. Turn under the neckline edges to match curve of neckline. Pin into place. Proceed to the next page ...

Turn the sweatshirt inside out and cut away the fleece fabric between the stitching lines. Next, stitch the top edges of fabric placket into place by hand or machine. If sewing by machine, stitch from the right side of the sweatshirt to maintain neat, controlled stitching.

You may wish to line the back of this zipper placket. A lining will provide a neater look and more stability. Cut 2 fabric strips slightly longer and wider than the original strips cut for the sides of the zipper. Turn back the edges on all sides of the strips and then pin into place on the inside of the shirt on each side of the back of the zipper. Sew strips in place by hand or if you choose to sew by machine, stitch from the front of the placket, making sure with careful pinning to catch the lining pieces in back.

A removable fabric facing can be added to the inside of the sweatshirt. The shirt could then be worn with the zipper open and the fabric facing would show behind the zipper. Cut 2 pieces of fabric the length of the zipper placket and slightly wider. Sew together with right sides of fabric inside and leave an inch free of stitching. Pull right sides out and seal the opening with fusible webbing or stitching.

Stitch small pieces of Velcro on each side of the facing piece. Sew the matching Velcro pieces onto the edges of sweatshirt fabric inside the shirt. By making this facing piece adjustable and removable, you can also pull the sweatshirt over your head — an important detail to arrange.

Other options:
1. Use decorative woven braid instead of fabric for sides and bottom of zipper.
2. Create a zipper front cardigan sweatshirt. Purchase a separating zipper as long as center front on the shirt or slightly shorter.

Decorating with Scissors

Sweatshirt fleece will not ravel or disintegrate along a cut edge. You can take advantage of this feature and decorate sweatshirts by simply cutting a design from the shirt.

One simple method is to draw a design on the shirt with a washable marker and then cut out the pieces of the design. Small shapes are recommended so the shirt will not become distorted as it is worn and washed. Stencil designs can often be used for patterns.

Another way to cut from a sweatshirt is to reinforce the fleece and the edges of the design before cutting. Use a lightweight fusible interfacing with stretch. (I like "Easy Knit" by Stacy.) Cut the interfacing larger than the design area. Use a pinking shears to prevent an "edge" from showing on the right side of the shirt. Fuse the interfacing on the fleece side of the shirt beneath the chosen design placement area. With a washable marker, draw the design to be cut away on the right side of the sweatshirt fabric. Sew around the design shapes with a straight stitch, using small stitches. Poke scissor tip through the sweatshirt inside the stitching lines and neatly cut away the fabric. With this method, the edge of the fleece is stabilized with stitching and the interfacing.

Placement of cut-away designs needs careful consideration, particularly for women's shirts. An upper center front placement is usually a good choice, as is the sleeve. The effect of a turtleneck shirt or blouse worn under the sweatshirt and showing beneath the cut-away areas can be effective and interesting.

Reverse Applique

If you would like the look of applique without doing the satin stitch around the shapes _or_ if your sewing machine does not zigzag, try this method of reverse applique. It is a simple and

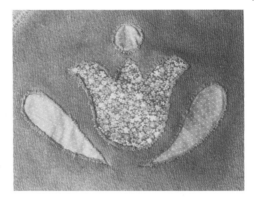

quick method. You will be stitching fabric onto the fleece side of the sweatshirt and then cutting away the fleece to reveal the fabric beneath.

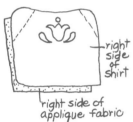

First select a design and cut pieces of fabric slightly larger than each part of the design. If the fabric is calico or other soft cotton, fuse lightweight interfacing to the back of the fabric for additional stability and smoothness.

Draw or trace a design on the right side of sweatshirt fabric. Place right side of applique fabric against fleece side of sweatshirt. Center beneath the area of design location. Pin into place. Stitch on the right side of the shirt all around design shape drawn on the shirt. Use a straight stitch. Carefully insert the scissors through the sweatshirt fleece ONLY and cut away the design shape inside the stitching line, thereby exposing the fabric below.

right side of shirt

right side of applique fabric

wrong side of sweatshirt

wrong side of applique fabric with interfacing

On the back or fleece side of the sweatshirt, you may wish to trim away some of the excess applique fabric. Leave at least ½" of fabric around the stitching. Use pinking shears, if available.

This method creates an appliqued look with a ridge of sweatshirt fabric outlining the design. With this approach, you can eliminate satin or applique stitching around design shapes.

(Hint: Simple designs seem to work best with this method.)

Free Machine Embroidery

Here's an interesting way to turn your sewing machine into an artistic instrument for decorating sweatshirts. With a few simple adjustments, you can set your machine to sew in any direction and you will be able to create drawings with the stitching.

Before you begin, give some tender loving care to your machine. Clean out the dust and oil it properly. Put in a new size 14 needle. 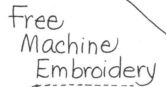 Begin with normal tension settings and adjust if you need to after practice sewing.

1. Remove the regular presser foot and use either no foot at all (my choice) or a darning foot which has a round hole in its center. You may find the darning foot will hold your work more securely and protect your fingers too.

2. Lower the feed dog so it will not move the fabric for you as you sew. Check the machine manual to determine if you do this by covering the feed dog with a plate or by adjusting a dial on the machine.

3. Set stitch length adjustment at 0.

4. Practice on a piece of sweatshirt fabric. Beneath the fabric pin a piece of tear-away stabilizer (such as Stitch N Tear Pellon®). Pull both top and bobbin threads back behind the needle.

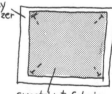

tear away stabilizer

sweatshirt fabric

Place the fabrics under the needle and LOWER THE PRESSER FOOT LEVER, even if you are not using a presser foot. This will be a step that is easy to forget. If you do forget, you will quickly have a wad of thread below the fabric and the machine will not work smoothly. Obviously, something is wrong!

top of fabric

ugly mess of thread!
Stop - cut threads - start again

Begin to stitch and move the fabric yourself. With some practice you will be able to adjust the speed of your movements and develop a relaxed free spirit to your stitching ～ Whoopee ～ Experiment with a zig-zag stitch or stitching back and forth over and over to fill in an area of a design.

When you have gained the confidence to begin free machining on your sweatshirt, draw your own design on your shirt with a washable marker or trace an applique design. Select a thread color to match or contrast with the sweatshirt color. Be sure to pin the tear away stabilizer behind the design area on the fleece side of the sweatshirt. As you stitch and follow the design, don't worry about stitching off the lines. Sew over the outline a second or third time, if you wish, stitching near the first seam. The look will be very artistic and interesting. Stitch your initials near the design to autograph your work of art. Combine this free embroidery with applique to add dimensions and details to the designs.

If you feel ambitious, pull the top threads to the back and tie knots or simply cut the thread "tails" from the front.

Removing the stabilizer from the back of the shirt is the next step and definitely not the most fun part of this project. Remove as much as you can, use a seam ripper to help you dig out the narrow small pieces, and then leave the rest. The stabilizer will soften with time and wear and should not prove to be a problem.

A good reference book with more information and ideas: Machine Embroidery with Style by dj Bennett.

3 paisley shapes (from page 57) were traced onto the shirt. I stitched around the shapes first and then filled in the centers with more stitching.

My thanks to Lois Mattson for her machine embroidery class and encouragement.

Appliques Around the Neck

A circle of applique designs around the neckline of a sweatshirt forms attractive trim for both the front and back of a shirt. For this alteration, the neck ribbing and a small part of the upper sweatshirt are removed after designs are stitched on.

The first step will be to select a design to use around the neckline. One repeated motif, like the bow on this page, or a variety may be used to outline the neck edge. Mark a ring around the neckline by placing marks 1" below the bottom of the neck ribbing. This is the line at which you will place the top edges of the applique shapes. (Placing the shapes much lower on the sweatshirt will produce a very large, open neckline. Be careful!) Measure around this new neckline marking with the tapemeasure on edge for an accurate measurement. Now you can determine the size and amount of applique shapes you will need to encircle the neckline. (Don't cut the shirt yet!)

Cut out shapes from fabric and fuse them into place around the neck. Use the applique stitch to sew the designs onto the shirt. Use a sharp scissor and cut away the ribbing and fabric above the appliques. Do not cut into stitching & leave a very small amount of sweatshirt fabric above the stitching line. And now you have a flattering "ring around the collar."

dashed lines indicate stitching lines.

Squeakers

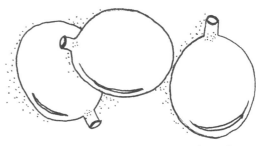

Plastic squeakers are available for use with appliques and they add a "musical" feature to your designs. These squeakers are especially popular for children's appliques but they can also be used for adults -- in the spirit of fun and surprises.

Squeakers are thin plastic "air bladders" which, when pressed, emit a squeak through a narrow neck end. When stitched into applique designs, they survive washing and drying in automatic machines at moderate temperatures.

Here's how: Cut a piece of applique fabric an inch or so wider and longer than the squeaker. Place the squeaker on the sweatshirt with the fabric piece over the top. With the zipper foot on the sewing machine, stitch the fabric onto the shirt close to the squeaker. Trim away the excess fabric close to the stitching line.

Hint: Select an applique design a good amount larger than the squeaker so you won't struggle with sewing the applique over the squeaker.

The squeaker will now be held in place on the garment. Over the top you will position and sew the applique shape. Use a gluestick to help hold the fabric in place. The finished applique will not be flat, but having a squeaker beneath the design will add charm and interest.

Consider the possibilities: How about a squeaky tomato or apple on the front of a butcher apron? A squeaker under a big round "Panic Button"? What about adult gag gifts? For matching mother-child sweatshirts, place a squeaker behind a Scottie dog on each shirt. I am sure you can devise some great ideas of your own.

Press Here
Panic Button

My thanks to Sharon Kerssen of Kerssen Originals (405 21st Ave. N., South St. Paul, MN 55075) for introducing me to squeakers and their possibilities.

Wooden Trims
a stand-out feature for a sweatshirt

Add a new dimension to your sweatshirt with light-weight wooden shapes. These wooden trims come in a variety of shapes and sizes and are available in craft shops. You can use narrow ribbon ties or Velcro to attach these light pieces to your shirt.

In order to attach the shapes with narrow ribbon or braid, two small holes must be drilled through the shape. You may wish to paint the shapes to add details and interest. Use acrylic paints and seal dried paint with a varnish coat. Next, position the shape on the shirt. Mark the location of the holes. Sew the ribbon or braid onto the sweatshirt very securely in the space between the holes. Then thread the ribbon ends through the holes in the shape and tie in a knot or bow on the front. (Large decorative buttons can also be attached in the same way.)

Velcro stitched on shirt →

If you plan to use Velcro for attaching the shape, glue one side of the Velcro to the back of the wooden shape, using household cement or other strong glue. Stitch the second side of the Velcro to the sweatshirt at the place you wish to locate the shape.

back of shape

Velcro

Have fun wearing your shirt with its new dimension! When it's time to launder it, remove the wooden shapes. Tie or stick them back on when the shirt is clean and dry.

Find many interesting wooden shapes at your favorite craft store.

Sweatshirt Vests

A   B   C

Simple pullover vests made of sweatshirt fleece have become popular leisure-wear garments. For many people, vests offer warmth and comfort for the upper body without fabric bulk or extra warmth in sleeves. Decorate vests in the same ways you decorate sweatshirts.

Vest A (above): Add plackets or snap tape along the shoulder seams. These openings add interesting detail and make the vest easier to get on and off. A woman who does not like to mess her hairdo will find this to be an attractive feature on a vest or sweatshirt.

Vest B : Shorten and/or "dress up" the bottom of a vest by cutting off the ribbing and turning up the bottom edge of the vest to form a casing. Stitch around the casing and cut a small hole in the center front of the casing. Pull a ribbon or braid through the opening and around the vest. Tie in a bow in the front.

Vest C : Make the vest a cardigan by stitching in plackets down the front. (For instructions, see page 13 of _Designer Sweatshirts_.) Use buttons or snaps to close the front.

Make a fashion "statement" by coordinating a vest with a blouse or turtleneck shirt. Use the colors or fabric of the shirt to decorate the vest.

Karen's wearing a cardigan vest with a coordinating print turtleneck shirt.

More Ideas for Lettuce Edging...

A ruffled or lettuce edge on the ribbing of sweatshirt necks and cuffs has become a popular feminine decoration. (See "Jackie's Lettuce Edge" on page 15 of DESIGNER SWEATSHIRTS.)

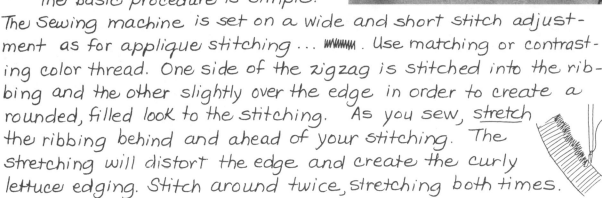

The basic procedure is simple. The sewing machine is set on a wide and short stitch adjustment as for applique stitching ... wwwww. Use matching or contrasting color thread. One side of the zigzag is stitched into the ribbing and the other slightly over the edge in order to create a rounded, filled look to the stitching. As you sew, <u>stretch</u> the ribbing behind and ahead of your stitching. The stretching will distort the edge and create the curly lettuce edging. Stitch around twice, stretching both times.

For an additional use of lettuce edging, consider a lettuce edge yoke. Place marks at frequent intervals around the neck. For a child, 4" from the bottom of the ribbing would be a suitable measure. For a woman, 6" or 7" would be appropriate. Pin a fold around the shirt with the marks on the crease of the fold. Sew on this fold as on the edge of the ribbing by stretching ahead and behind the sewing machine needle. Stitch around twice. You could add more rows of edging spaced at different intervals or vary the measurement around the yoke to create a deeper "dip" in the front. A small appliqued or cross-stitched design in the center front of the yoke could be added.

Another possibility for lettuce edging is to place the stitching in the middle of the neckband rather than at the top. Mark the center of the band all around the ribbing. Fold the ribbing at the marks, pulling the wrong side of the ribbing away from the fold. You will stretch and sew as before but on the front ribbing only. Stitching in this location creates the look of two neckbands.

Enjoy curling the edges on your sweatshirts, turtlenecks, anklets or any knit edge that will stretch.

More About Pockets

~Notes~

In DESIGNER SWEATSHIRTS, pockets on sweatshirt sleeves were presented as a decorative touch to the shirt. Of course this is not the only place to locate a pocket. For a more useful pocket, position a pocket shape on the body of the sweatshirt.

For a woman who likes to keep her keys or kleenex handy, one pocket at the shirt bottom above the ribbing is convenient. Make sure you place it according to whether she is right or left handed. The pocket can be any shape from square to that of a large strawberry or heart.

Hint: Line pockets with interfacing or use double fabric so pockets will maintain their shape + not "droop" with use.

A handwarmer pocket can be added to the bottom center front of a sweatshirt. The pocket shown has 2 zippers. For an adult, this pocket could be approximately 9" x 13". The zippers can be sewed to the pocket fabric before the pocket is sewed onto the sweatshirt. Turn back and iron the raw edges on all 4 sides of the pocket piece. Center and pin securely to shirt before stitching.

For a handwarmer pocket similar to those found on hooded sweatshirts, cut curved sections away from a 9" x 13" rectangle. Make sure a hand could fit through the curved opening. Cut 2 pockets from fabric. Place right sides together and stitch around the shape, leaving a small opening through which you will turn the pocket right side out. Seal the opening by handstitching or fusible webbing. Position and stitch the pocket onto the shirt. (Don't forget to leave the pocket openings free of stitching!)

When you select pocket fabrics, remember that a pocket of brightly colored contrasting fabric will be an eye-catching spot on the sweatshirt. For a person with a prominent stomach, consider using a solid color to match the shirt. Be very aware that any decorative addition to the shirt is where the observer's eye will be drawn.

PLACKETS

designer sweatshirts showed you how to construct a traditional size placket in a simple way. Now let's expand the idea to create W-I-D-E-R plackets for a new look.

The method of construction will be the same, but now the pattern is increased in size. The finished placket will be approximately 4" wide.

Before stitching up the sides of the placket, trim away most of the excess sweatshirt fabric rather than tuck it all inside the placket.

To close the placket you can use 2 "D" rings and ribbon. Sew "D" rings onto a ribbon tab on the placket. Sew a longer strip of ribbon onto the shirt to the side of the placket.

This placket can also be worn open for a more casual look.

You can also consider constructing a very narrow and shorter placket with fabric or ribbon ties as closures.

← 4" →

Still More Ideas

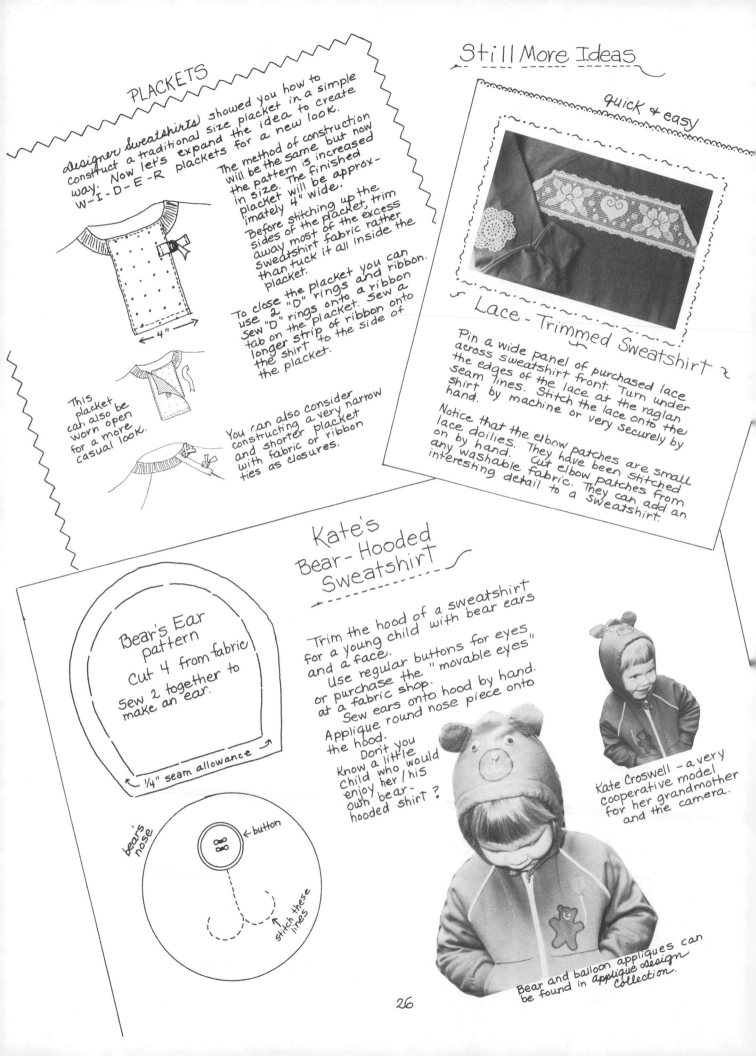

Lace-Trimmed Sweatshirt

Pin a wide panel of purchased lace across sweatshirt front. Turn under the edges of the lace at the raglan seam lines. Stitch the lace onto the shirt by machine or very securely by hand.

Notice that the elbow patches are small lace doilies. They have been stitched on by hand. Cut elbow patches from any washable fabric. They can add an interesting detail to a sweatshirt.

Kate's Bear-Hooded Sweatshirt

Bear's Ear Pattern
Cut 4 from fabric
Sew 2 together to make an ear.

← ¼" seam allowance

bear's nose

← button

stitch these lines →

Trim the hood of a sweatshirt for a young child with bear ears and a face.

Use regular buttons for eyes or purchase the "movable eyes" at a fabric shop.

Sew ears onto hood by hand. Applique round nose piece onto the hood.

Don't you know a little child who would enjoy her/his own bear-hooded shirt?

Kate Croswell – a very cooperative model for her grandmother and the camera.

Bear and balloon appliques can be found in *applique design collection*.

26

Choices to Make

* This is an important page - please pay attention.

We have some important choices to make as we create designer sweatshirts for women - choices in fabrics, design size, and placement.

Selecting fabrics for shirt trims can be a challenge and an obstacle. Many "busy" print fabrics on a shirt tend to detract from the charm and total effect of the decorations. Pin dot fabrics are usually an excellent choice. They are available in a rainbow of color selections and can be used together well or combined effectively with busy calico prints. Solid color fabrics can also be used. If you don't trust your judgment, remember that fewer mistakes are made with pin-dots and solid colors. To paraphrase Will Rogers: "I never saw a pin-dot applique I didn't like."

a pin-dot heart

Design size needs to be considered. Large size designs cover more area and choices of where to locate them become limited once the shirt is placed on a woman's body. Repeating a smaller design 3 or 5 times across

the sweatshirt upper front can be pleasing to the eye, easy to do, and effective. Artists and designers emphasize that an odd number is more pleasing to the eye than an even number. We need to remember this as we design sweatshirts.

It is best to consider the sweatshirt not as a flat, blank canvas to be trimmed at random, but as a garment with dimensions. These dimensions are best noted when the shirt is worn on a body. If the bustline or stomach are prominent features, you may want to keep attention away from those areas. Any area decorated is where the eye of the viewer will be drawn. One "neutral" area for most women is the upper chest area, above the bustline and around the shirt neckline. Designs in this area draw the viewer's eye from the design to the face and do not pinpoint figure flaws.

Other comments and suggestions for design placement can be found in Designer Sweatshirts.

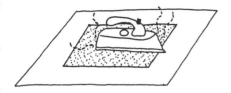

Preparing Appliques – Two Methods

Industry and the space program have invented products we can use for sewing and decorating garments. Velcro is one of these products. Another is Teflon® which is used for applique pressing sheets. Here's the first method to speed up and improve applique preparation with an applique pressing sheet:

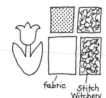

fabric   Stitch Witchery

1. Select an applique design and fabrics for each part of the design. Cut a piece of fabric slightly larger than each design part. Cut a piece of fusible webbing (Stitch Witchery or Fine Fuse) slightly smaller than each fabric piece.

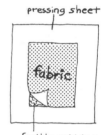

pressing sheet

fabric

fusible webbing

2. Place the pressing sheet flat on the ironing board. Place fusible webbing on top of the sheet. Place the fabric, right side up, over the webbing. Set the iron on "steam" and "wool." With a press and lift motion, hold the iron down for 10 seconds in each area of the fabric. You may use a press cloth on top of the fabric. (This is recommended for specialty fabrics such as Ultrasuede.)

3. Let the fabric cool for a few seconds before peeling it away from the pressing sheet. You will notice that the back of the fabric is now slick and shiny. The fusible webbing has melted to the fabric but is still usable for one more step in this applique procedure.

end of stem goes under tulip

4. Place the applique pattern on the right side of the treated fabric. Pin in place and cut around or trace and cut. If the design has many pieces, cut a 1/8" underlap on one piece where two design pieces meet.

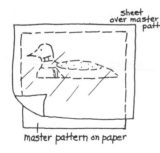

sheet over master pattern

master pattern on paper

5. To assemble a design with many pieces, use the pressing sheet to help you align all the pieces. Lay the sheet over the paper pattern. Since you can see through the sheet, you can position all fabric pieces correctly on top of the sheet. (Remember that some pieces have a 1/8" underlap to be placed beneath adjoining design parts.) Carefully press the design pieces together with the iron. Allow to cool and then peel the entire design from the sheet. (Store the sheet for use over and over again.)

Design parts traced onto Wonder-Under ™

The second method of preparing appliques makes use of Wonder-Under ™, special paper backed with fusible webbing.

1. Trace the design pieces on the paper side of Wonder-Under ™, remembering to reverse the design if it has a direction as some alphabet letters do. Add a 1/8" extension to the pieces to be placed under other parts of the design.

2. Press the Wonder-Under ™ with the traced design (paper side up) to the wrong side of the applique fabric. Cut out the design and peel off the paper backing.

Both Methods: Use the following steps to position applique designs.

A. Place the applique design pieces in position on the garment or item to be decorated. Pin them in place and TRY ON THE GARMENT and inspect carefully. Adjust the pieces if needed before fusing the designs in place by pressing and holding the iron down for 10 seconds on each part of the design.

Before you sew the applique in place, pin a piece of tearaway stabilizer such as Stitch 'N Tear Pellon on the wrong side of the garment, beneath the design. This product will help you to create smooth applique stitching. (For more detailed applique stitching instructions, see _Designer Sweatshirts_, page 18-19.)

The two methods for preparing appliques have the advantage of producing applique pieces which can be pressed securely in place and fused down all the way to the edges. Frayed edges are no longer a problem. This bonded placement will make sewing with the applique stitch easier.

You can also produce your own iron-on patches with either the applique pressing sheet or Wonder-Under ™. Of course, sewing repairs aren't nearly as much fun as sewing appliques, but sometimes we have to tend to "maintenance" sewing too.

The Ever-Overflowing Mending Basket

Mary's Maxims

Ideas and Suggestions distilled from many years of observations, experience, teaching, and also my personal opinions.

Some fabric and sweatshirt colors that always seem to look good to-gether are navy blue, red, & kelly green.

Consider the personality and tastes of the person who will wear the garment. What would be most ap-propriate? Bold? Subtle?

would this be "pressed duck"?

Any applique or fabric added to a sweatshirt will look much better if it is ironed <u>after</u> the shirt is laundered.

designer sweatshirt care label

If you are making designer sweatshirts for others, write care labels and include instructions on how to launder and care for the shirt. Recommend pressing after laundering. The person who receives this special shirt from you will appreciate your laundering "guidelines."

Please don't do this to a sweatshirt!

We may laugh but it seems to be so easy to place prominent designs "on target" on the bustline. Try to avoid placing appliques like these 2 hearts level with the "armpits" of the shirt.

∴ A Good Motto is ∴

Keep It Simple

If you are excited about making "designer sweatshirts," control yourself as you select applique designs. Limit your-self to one or two designs per shirt. The effect will be much more charming than this shirt.

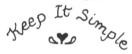

Remember that pindots are great applique fabrics.

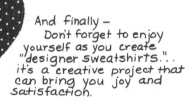

And finally —
Don't forget to enjoy yourself as you create "designer sweatshirts.". . it's a creative project that can bring you joy and satisfaction.

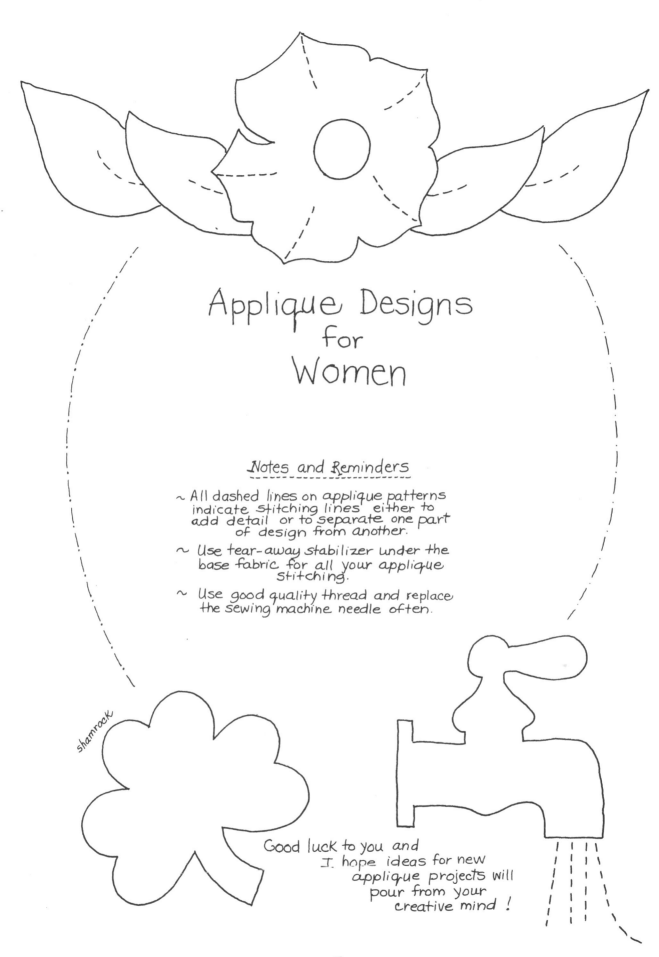

Applique Designs
for
Women

Notes and Reminders

~ All dashed lines on applique patterns indicate stitching lines either to add detail or to separate one part of design from another.

~ Use tear-away stabilizer under the base fabric for all your applique stitching.

~ Use good quality thread and replace the sewing machine needle often.

shamrock

Good luck to you and I hope ideas for new applique projects will pour from your creative mind !

Butterflies

Hot Air Balloon

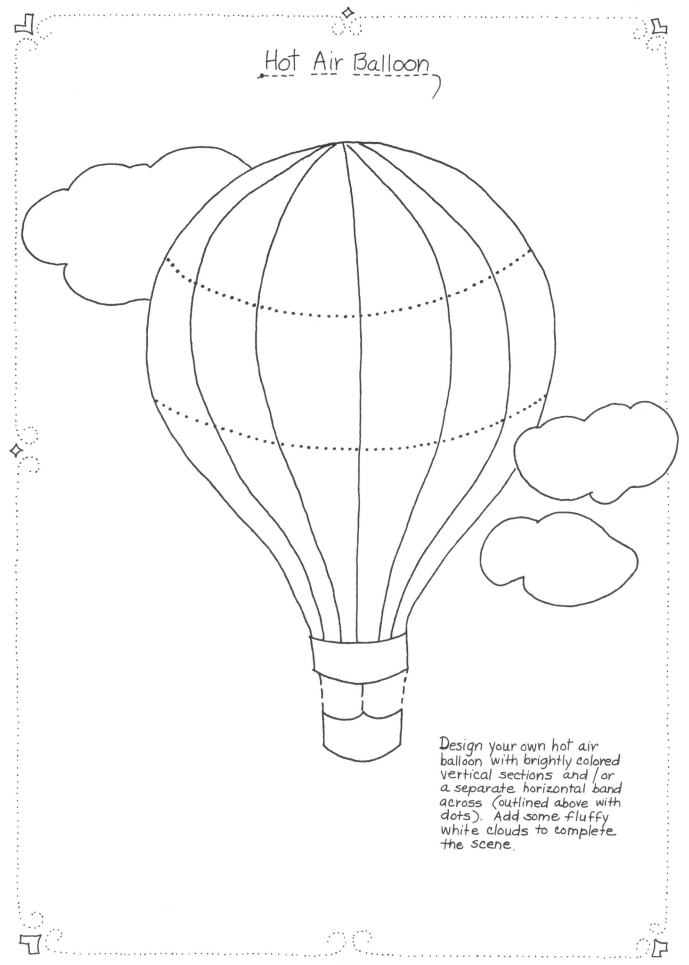

Design your own hot air balloon with brightly colored vertical sections and / or a separate horizontal band across (outlined above with dots). Add some fluffy white clouds to complete the scene.

cash . . .

. . . end-of-the season sales . . . cash

Spending money is a fun hobby . . .

buy, buy, buy . . . $ $ $ . . . Spending money . . .

. . . Spending money . . . sales . . . save money . . . shop . . .

Her motto: I was born to shop . . . shopping bags . . . $ and ¢ . . . shop locally . . . great savings today . . . rush in and buy . . . cash deals.

For the Shopper

Shop

$ale

price tag

an apron for a store clerk

Use these designs to decorate a shirt for a friend who loves to shop.

shop

Tote bags are fun to decorate and they make great gifts.

. . . the sale of the century . . . money, money, money . . . bargains galore . . . the buy of a lifetime . . .

34

Quilt Patterns

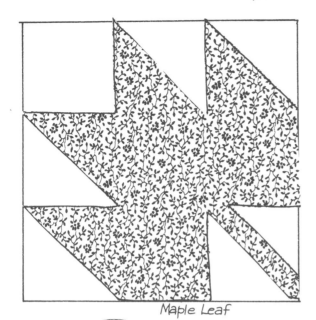

Maple Leaf

Pinwheel

3 Maple Leaf squares decorate a sweatshirt.

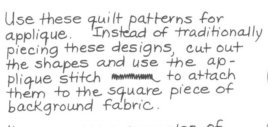

Use these quilt patterns for applique. Instead of traditionally piecing these designs, cut out the shapes and use the applique stitch ∿∿∿∿∿ to attach them to the square piece of background fabric.

Here are some examples of uses for these quilt patterns.

This pocket uses the fan pattern centered on a larger square of fabric.

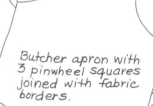

Butcher apron with 3 pinwheel squares joined with fabric borders.

Shoo-Fly

Fan

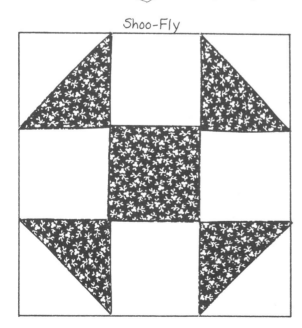

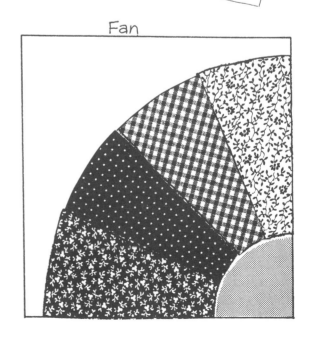

35

(Cupid was here)

Hearts

Heart Box

Arrange heart boxes in rows or stacks.

Heart in Hand —
a traditional 19th century symbol of love.

"If it's made by your hands, it comes from your heart."

...and More Hearts

Hearts are great symmetrical shapes for decorating. Have you guessed that they're my favorite shape?

37

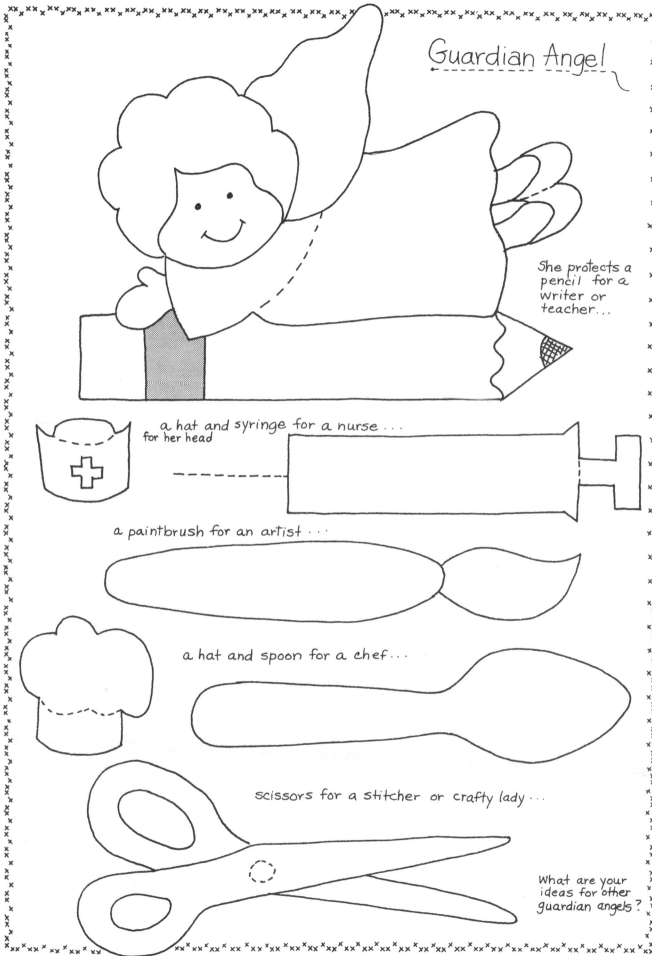

Guardian Angel

She protects a
pencil for a
writer or
teacher...

a hat and syringe for a nurse...
for her head

a paintbrush for an artist...

a hat and spoon for a chef...

scissors for a stitcher or crafty lady...

What are your
ideas for other
guardian angels?

38

Angels

Angels to:
~ announce glad tidings
~ decorate for Christmas
~ applique in a
    "country" theme

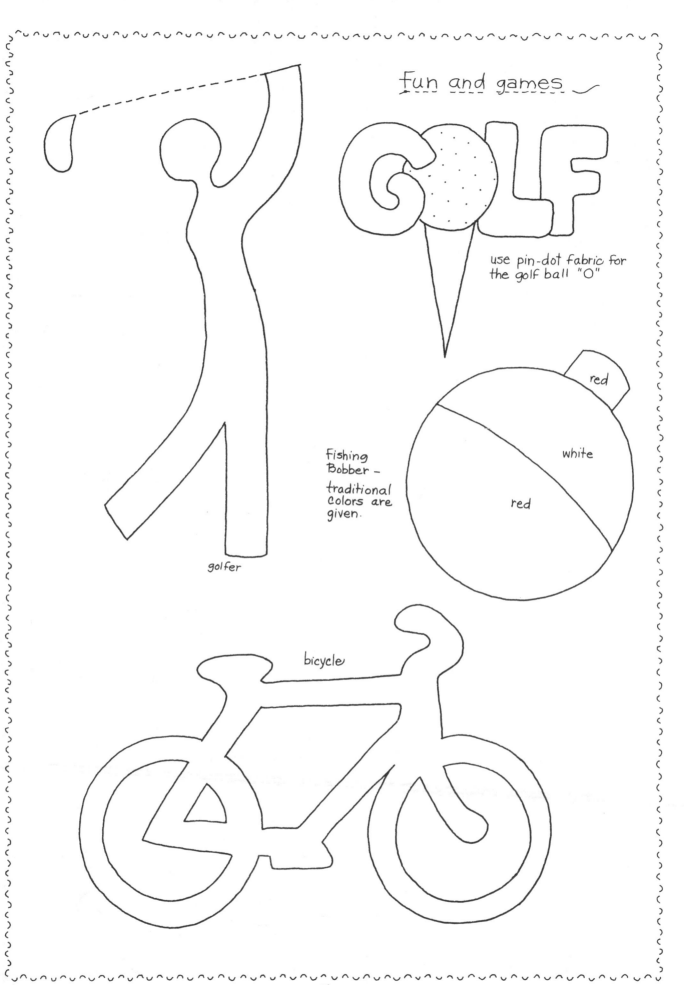

fun and games

GOLF

use pin-dot fabric for the golf ball "O"

golfer

Fishing Bobber — traditional colors are given.

red

white

red

bicycle

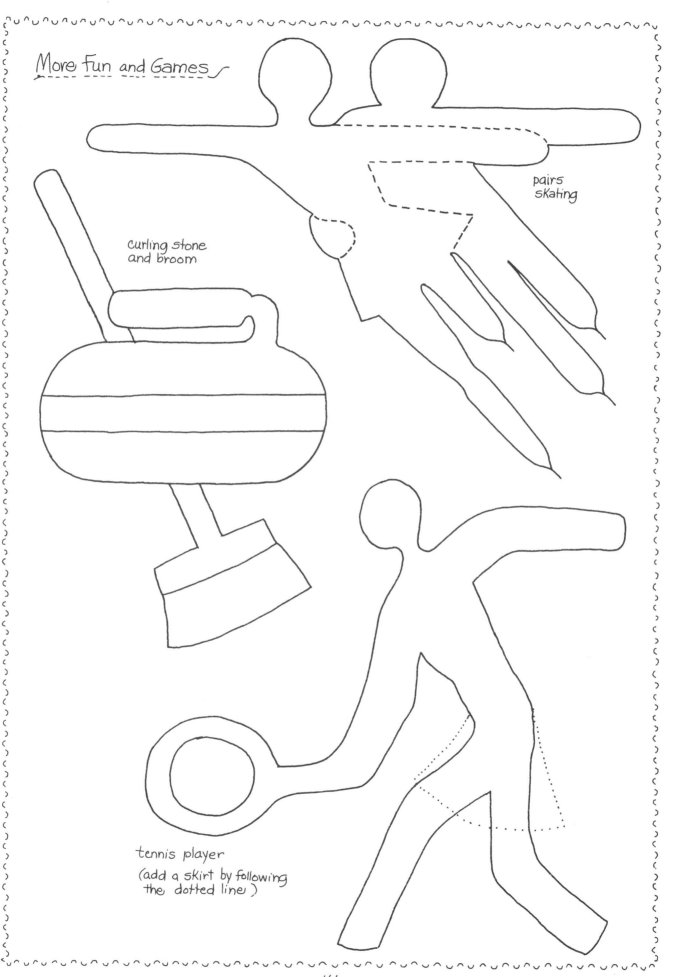

More Fun and Games

pairs skating

curling stone and broom

tennis player
(add a skirt by following the dotted line)

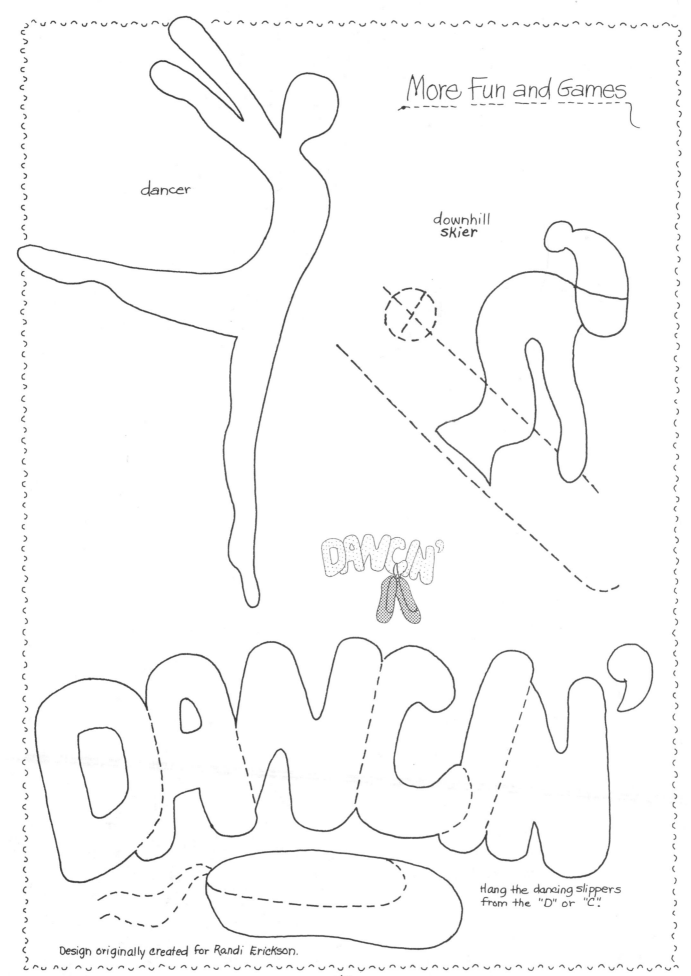

dancer

downhill skier

DANCIN'

DANCIN'

Hang the dancing slippers from the "D" or "C".

Design originally created for Randi Erickson.

Scandinavian Designs

Scandinavian
woven heart

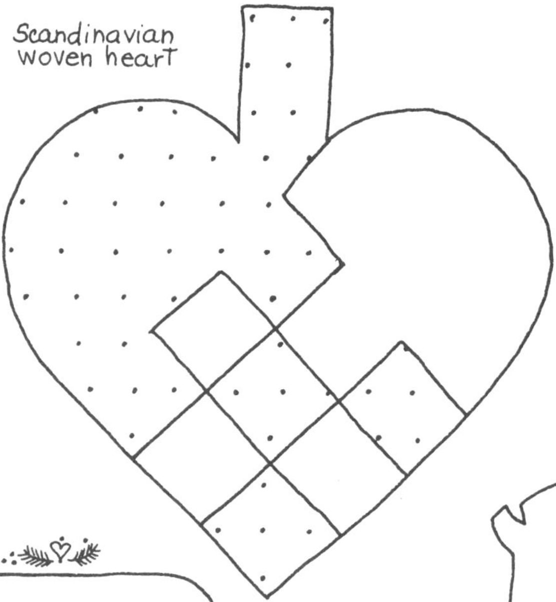

Nancy's wearing her
smock style apron
decorated with
3 woven hearts.
The apron is green
and the hearts
are red and white
so it's a great
apron for Christmas.
Nancy always rec-
ommends pin dot
fabrics for appliques.

Viking ship

Scandinavian
elves

(nisse or Tomte)

~ red bodies and hats
~ white beards
~ yellow blonde
   braids for the
   female

Flowers

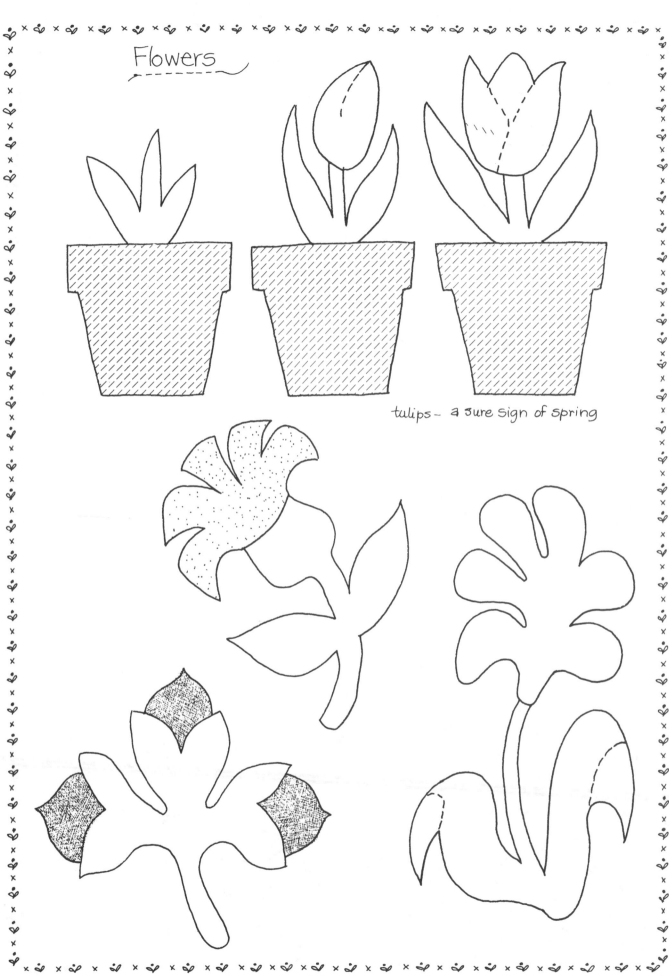

tulips— a sure sign of spring

Flowers

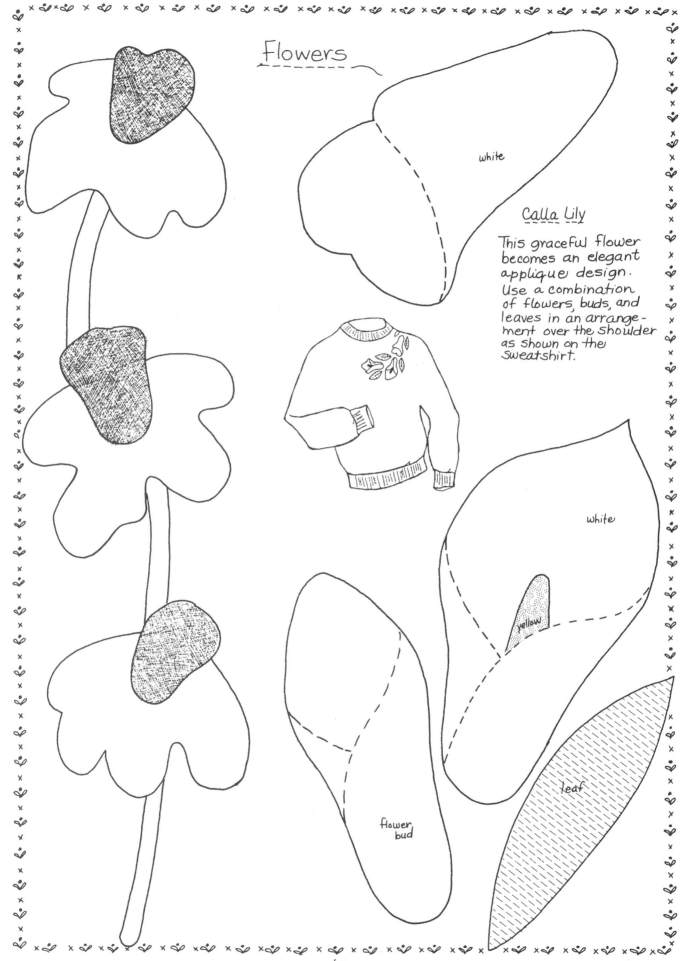

white

Calla Lily

This graceful flower becomes an elegant applique design. Use a combination of flowers, buds, and leaves in an arrangement over the shoulder as shown on the sweatshirt.

white

yellow

flower bud

leaf

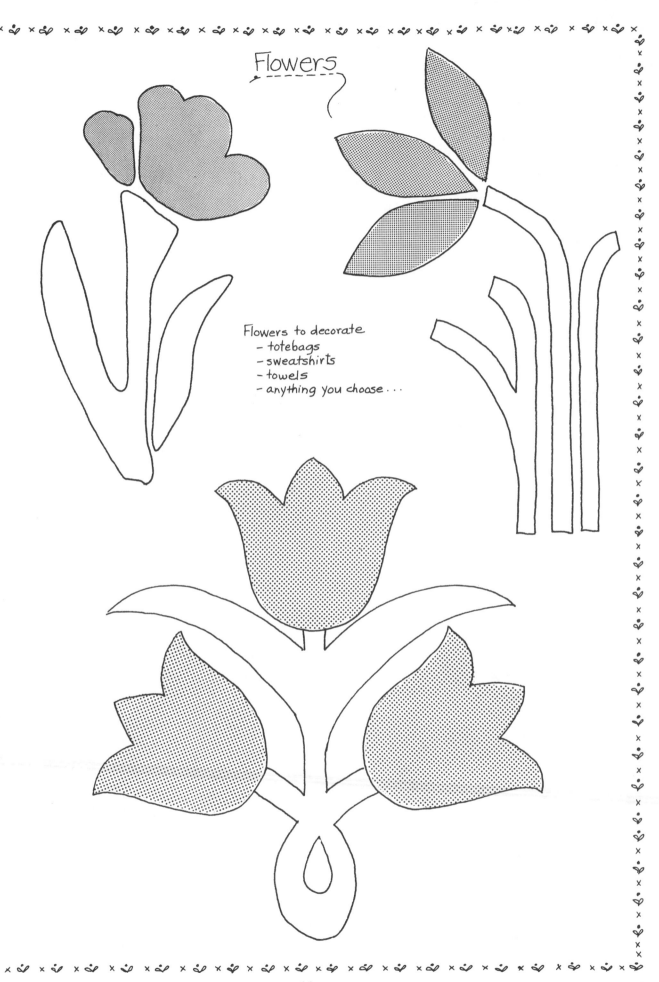

Flowers

Flowers to decorate
- totebags
- sweatshirts
- towels
- anything you choose...

Flowers

Iris

My favorite
apron style

Birds of a Feather...

hummingbird

red

white

Mary Jo's hint:
Use 3 small
buttons inside
this flower to add
interesting detail.

general all-purpose
bird

seagulls
wings may be
outlined with
gray thread

More Birds

Mallard

correct colors are noted.

dark green

gold

white

medium tan

rust

medium blue

black

white

light tan

back view of bird

Add eyes to birds with hand embroidery, machine stitching or teeny tiny buttons.

general all-purpose flying bird

school
bell

Dorothy is modeling a shirt she
decorated for her daughter who
is an elementary school teacher.
She used the "abc" and apple
designs and rickrack to
create a yoke around the
neckline.

envelopes to trim a
sweatshirt for a
mail carrier
or a
dedicated
letter
writer

a left-handed writer
(flip the design over if
you are right-handed)

Occupations and Interests

Beautician's tools

cards, anyone?

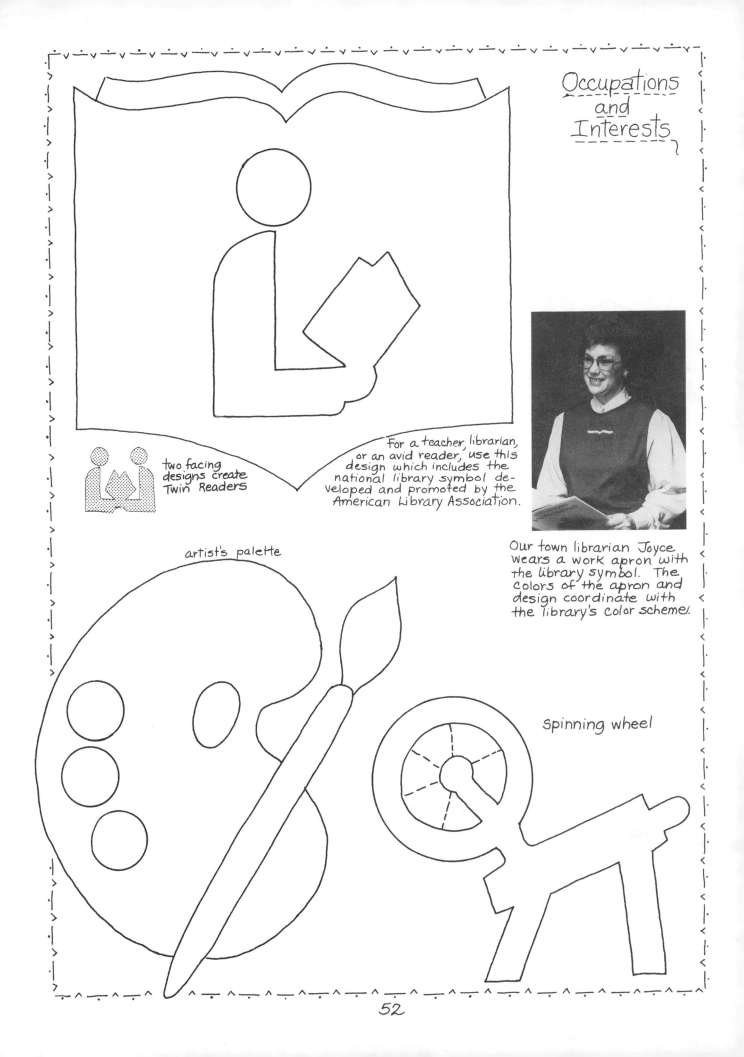

two facing
designs create
Twin Readers

For a teacher, librarian,
or an avid reader, use this
design which includes the
national library symbol developed and promoted by the
American Library Association.

Our town librarian Joyce
wears a work apron with
the library symbol. The
colors of the apron and
design coordinate with
the library's color scheme.

artist's palette

spinning wheel

52

Cats and Dogs

Stitch in eyes
and face details
by hand or machine
or use very tiny buttons.

Two Scotties

Use the larger
pattern (as
indicated with
dash and dot
line) if you
plan to stitch
a squeaker beneath
the applique.

Bow tie for larger Scottie

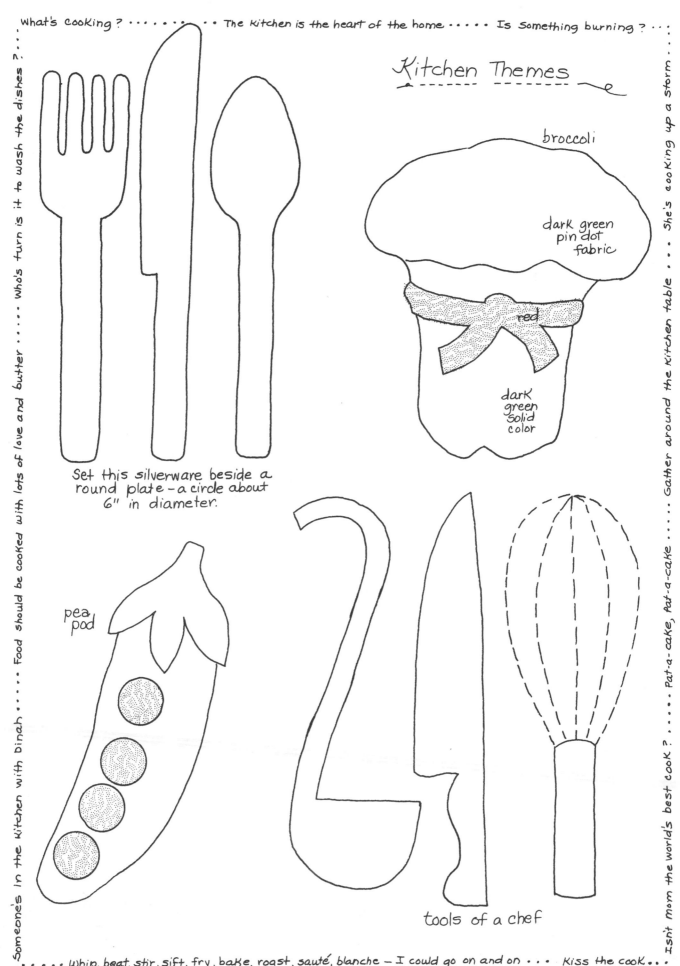

Kitchen Themes

broccoli

dark green pin dot fabric

red

dark green solid color

Set this silverware beside a round plate – a circle about 6" in diameter.

pea pod

tools of a chef

Who's turn is it to wash the dishes? . . .

Food should be cooked with lots of love and butter . . . . .

Someone's in the kitchen with Dinah . . . . .

Gather around the kitchen table . . . She's cooking up a storm . . .

. . . . Pat-a-cake, Pat-a-cake . . . . .

Isn't mom the world's best cook? . . . .

. . . . . Whip, beat, stir, sift, fry, bake, roast, sauté, blanche – I could go on and on . . . Kiss the cook . . .

54

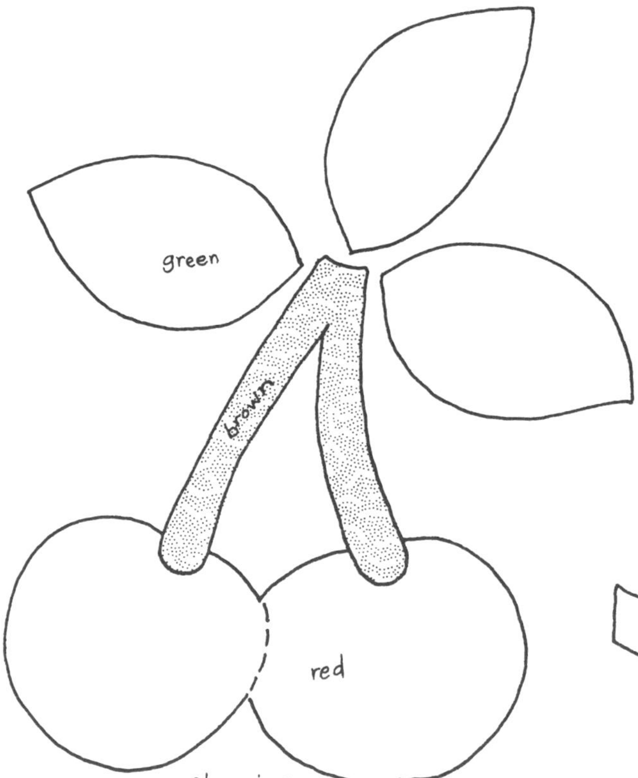

green

brown

red

Cherries

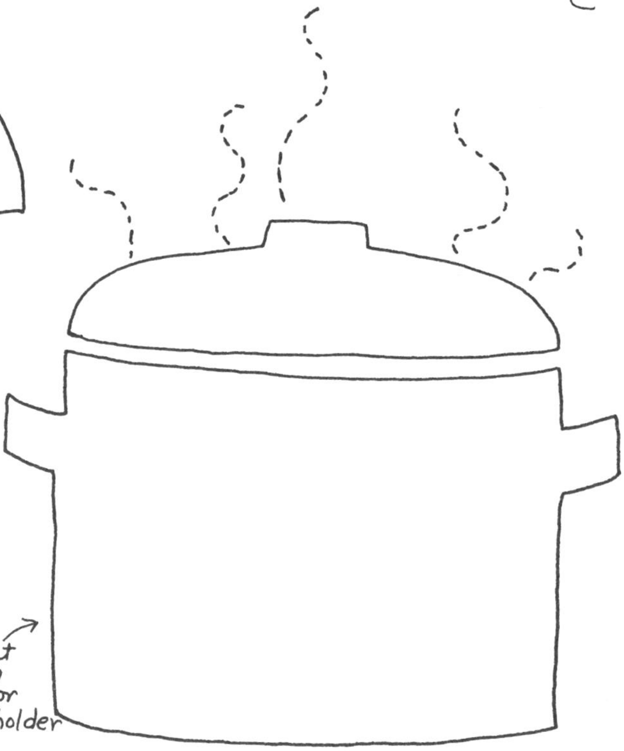

Kitchen Themes Again

a great
design
idea for
a potholder

a hot pot –
stitch steam lines
curling above the lid

a pair of country geese
for your country kitchen

"Beatrice"

"Lester"

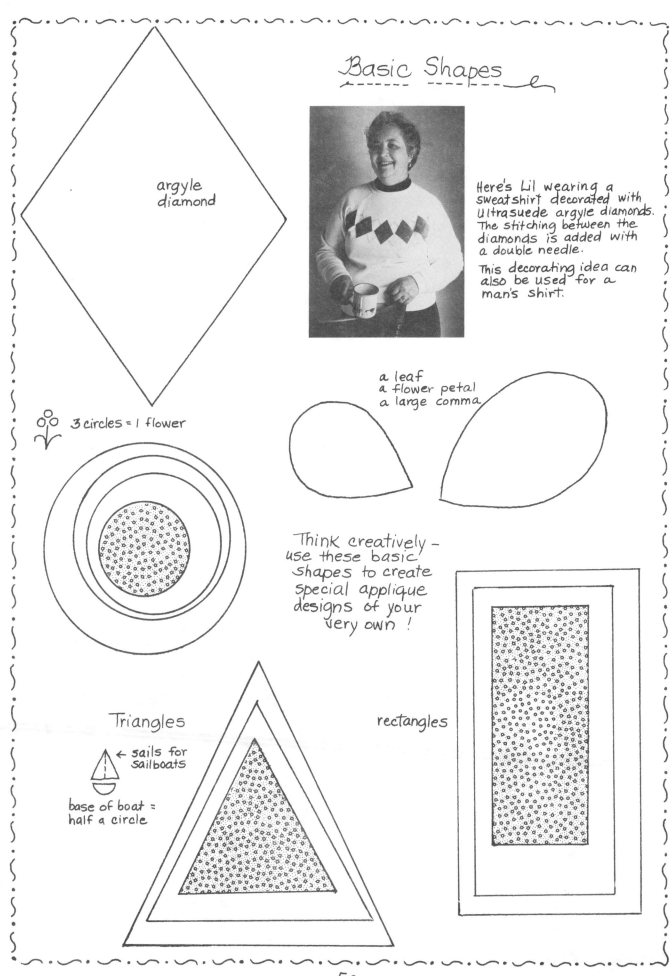

Basic Shapes

argyle diamond

Here's Lil wearing a sweatshirt decorated with Ultrasuede argyle diamonds. The stitching between the diamonds is added with a double needle.

This decorating idea can also be used for a man's shirt.

3 circles = 1 flower

a leaf
a flower petal
a large comma

Think creatively — use these basic shapes to create special applique designs of your very own!

Triangles

← sails for sailboats

base of boat = half a circle

rectangles

Basic Shapes

paisley shapes
(or leaves)

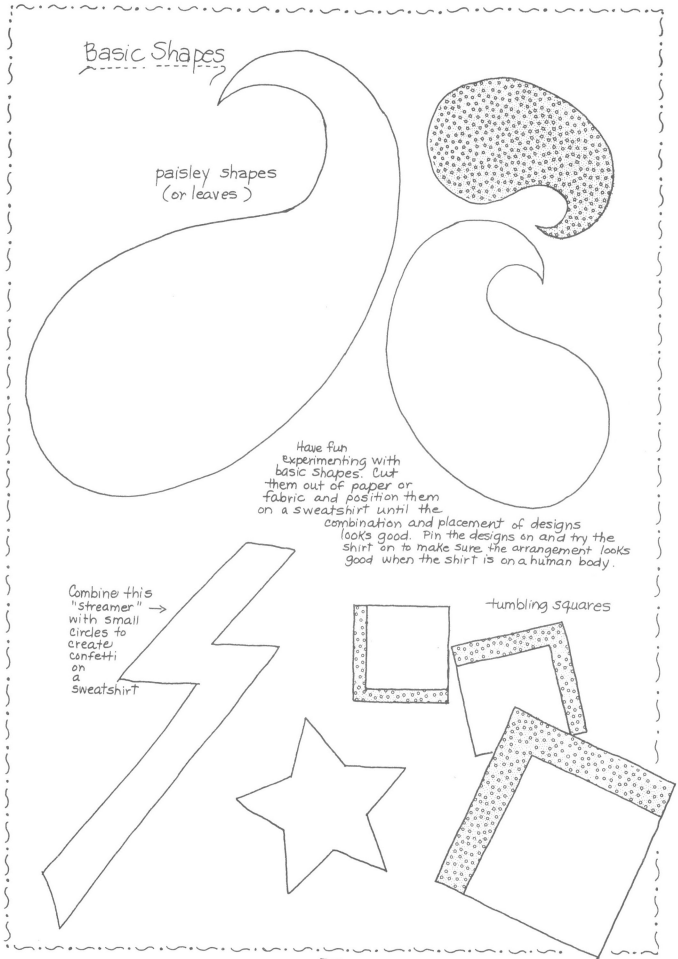

Have fun
experimenting with
basic shapes. Cut
them out of paper or
fabric and position them
on a sweatshirt until the
combination and placement of designs
looks good. Pin the designs on and try the
shirt on to make sure the arrangement looks
good when the shirt is on a human body.

Combine this
"streamer" →
with small
circles to
create
confetti
on
a
sweatshirt

tumbling squares

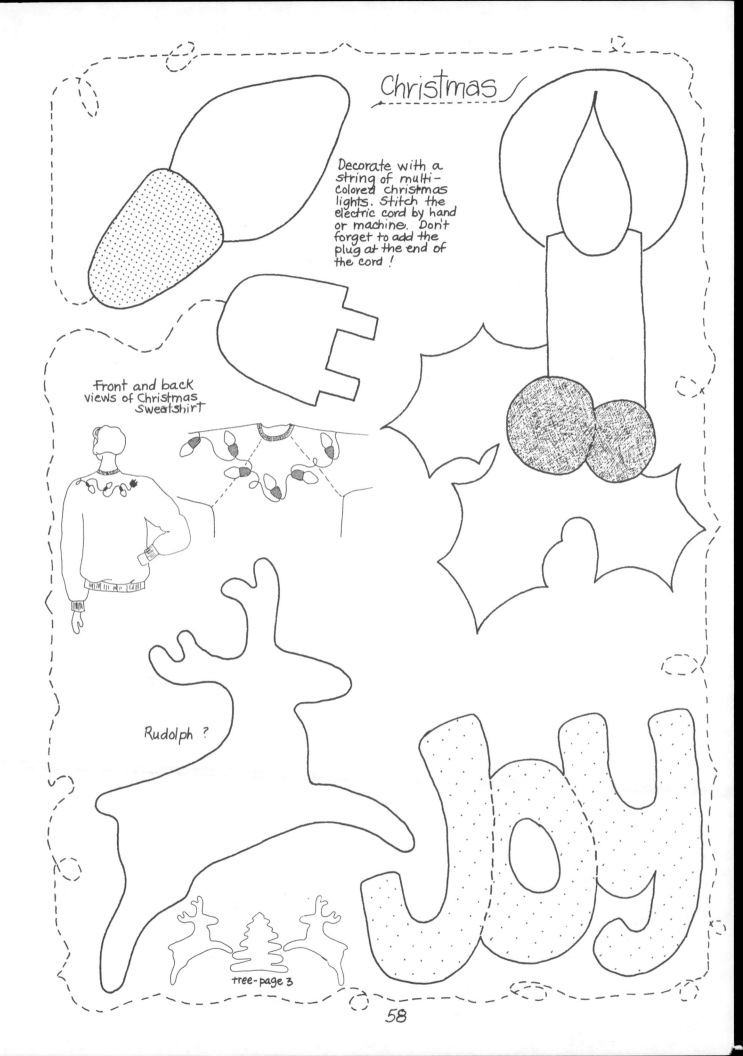

Decorate with a string of multi-colored christmas lights. Stitch the electric cord by hand or machine. Don't forget to add the plug at the end of the cord !

Front and back views of Christmas Sweatshirt

Rudolph ?

tree-page 3

JOY

Index of Applique Designs

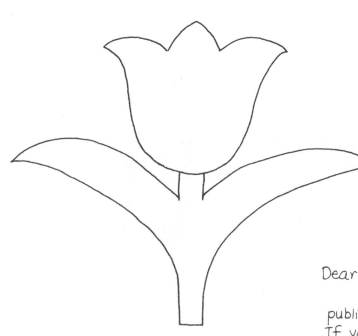

Books by Mary Mulari

Designer Sweatshirts

Applique Design Collection

MORE Designer Sweatshirts

Country Style Appliques

Adventure in Applique

Accents for Your Style

Other Products

"Designer Sweatshirts" video
Minnesota Applique Designs folder
"Papers for Stitchers" notecards

Available from:

Mary's Productions
Box 87 - Dept. 103
Aurora, MN 55705

Dear Reader,

This is the third book published by Mary's Productions. If you are interested in the previously published books and designs or products mentioned in this book, please write to me. (Including a self-addressed stamped envelope with your request will bring you a speedy reply.) I really enjoy hearing from readers so please do write!

Thank you for your interest in my books and ideas. I have been encouraged by your response to my work. In turn, I hope I have inspired you to creative efforts with sweatshirts and applique designs.

Sincerely,

Mary Mulari